Raelene Philip

Where Is Your Pineapple?

A HANDBOOK ON HOSPITALITY

RAELENE PHILLIPS

✢✢EvidentPress

Where Is Your Pineapple?

International Standard Book Number: 0-965049-3-2

For information:
Evident Press, L.L.C.
830 Kelsey St. NE
Grand Rapids, MI 49505
1.616.459.2882
www.evidentpress.com

Printed in the United States of America at:
Color House Graphics
Grand Rapids, MI
1.616.241.1916

Cover Design and Layout by Jim Hossler

This book is lovingly dedicated to the congregations of two wonderful churches who have taught me anew the **True** meaning of hospitality:

Newson Missionary Church
9310 Cowpath Road
St. Paris, OH 43072

and

Delaware Bible Church
45 Belle
Delaware, OH 43015
(especially Connie Cline)

Thank you to all of you.

TABLE OF CONTENTS

WHERE IS YOUR PINEAPPLE?

Have you ever seen a sculpture of a pineapple on a fence post at the end of a long lane leading to a lovely country home? Ever noticed an ornate pineapple on the newel post at the foot of a stairway? Or perhaps you have seen a pineapple carved into the casement above a door? Or as the center (spouting piece) in a beautiful fountain? In a small town near my home the top of the court house is bedecked with a brass pineapple. Ever wonder why you see pineapples everywhere? For, let me warn you…once you begin to notice, you will see them everywhere.

The tradition of decorating with pineapples dates back to the very earliest days of colonial America. The pineapple was relatively unknown in the New World. Only when traders began to bring them from islands whose climate allows their growth, did our forefathers learn of this delicious fruit. And it soon became a much-sought-after delicacy. It was a sign of affluence if a hostess could serve a pineapple to her guests. People felt that no expense had been spared to provide for their culinary delights when the meal was topped off with a few bites of pineapple.

Less affluent people could not afford pineapples. Still wanting their guests to feel special however, a hostess could opt to rent a pineapple with which to decorate her buffet table. Research shows that renting pineapples was a common practice in colonial America. Guests at a dinner party were often kept in suspense in a parlor until the special moment when a servant would open the doors to the dining room. "Oohs" and "ahs" abounded when guests spotted a pineapple amidst the other delectables on the buffet. Then, they would wait to see if the hostess would actually cut the fruit. If it was never cut, the astute guest surmised that the fruit had been rented, rather than purchased. Indeed, some pineapples were used as many as 5 times before a wealthier hostess would actually serve the fruit rather than just display it.

So, it came about that a pineapple became

a sign of hospitality. That is why architects incorporated them into so many different structures in earlier decades. That is also why, in any decorating or craft store, you can still find pineapples. You will see them on placemats, on pottery, on wallpaper, on clocks, on coasters, on picture-frames, on stationary…the list is endless. Our grandmothers learned to crochet the outlines of pineapples into tablecloths and bedspreads. Yes, pineapples are indeed everywhere.

Our forefathers often had a special replica of a pineapple made out of wrought iron, cement, or carved from wood. This pineapple was placed on their porch whenever they were willing to receive "callers" and removed from the porch if they did not wish to have guests. People came to understand that if the pineapple was visible the people in the house would welcome guests. If the pineapple was hidden, it would be better to visit some other time. So, it became a common thing to hear a neighbor call, "Where is your pineapple?"

With this background information, let me ask you, gentle reader, that same question. In light of Biblical teaching about hospitality…

WHERE IS YOUR PINEAPPLE?

CHAPTER 1

THE BIBLICAL MANDATE

I know many Christians who would answer the question with, "I don't even have a pineapple. Hospitality is not my thing."

Others would respond, "Well, if I had a pineapple, I couldn't afford to put it outside. I'd like to entertain people and show hospitality, but we can barely afford to feed ourselves. There is no way I can stretch the food budget to include having dinner parties."

Some would say, "Hospitality is one of the spiritual gifts given to believers. It is not the gift I received. I am a teacher (or I have the gift of prophecy or giving or… whatever). So I don't have to worry about where my pineapple is. I don't have that gift."

I know people who say, "People used to have folks over for meals at the drop of a hat. Back in the 'good old days' we were a much more hospitable society.   But nowadays we are just too busy to worry about where our pineapple is. Things used to be better."

In 1 Peter 4:8 & 9 (New Living Translation), the Holy Spirit tells us through the pen of the apostle Peter, "Continue to show deep love for each other, for love covers a multitude of sins. Cheerfully share your home with those who need a meal or a place to stay." In Romans12:13 (New Living Translation) Paul admonishes us with, "And get into the habit of inviting guests home for dinner or, if they need lodging, for the night." The Message renders that same verse with these words: "Be inventive in hospitality."

As I read these verses, I don't see that Christians have a choice in this matter of where to place our pineapples. The Bible does not tell us to show hospitality only if it is 'our thing'. Or if we have the money, if it is our spiritual gift, or if we are not too busy. It simply tells us to share our home! Get into the habit of inviting guests! Those do not sound like suggestions to me. It sounds as though this is a Biblical mandate.

CHAPTER 2

THE BLESSING

In the Old Testament, there is an interesting account of a woman who had her pineapple on the porch (figuratively speaking) in 2 Kings 4:8-10.

"One day Elisha went to the town of Shunem. A wealthy woman lived there and she invited him to eat some food. From then on, whenever he passed that way, he would stop there to eat.

She said to her husband, 'I am sure this man who stops in from time to time is a holy man of God. Let's make a little room for him on the roof and furnish it with a bed, a table, a chair, and a lamp. Then he will have a place to stay whenever he comes by.'"

The Biblical narrative continues to tell us that because she did this God blessed her with a son. I can envision that child coming home from his Hebrew lessons or from working in the field and seeing Elisha's donkey. He would probably excitedly say, "Oh look! The man of God is here!" And Elisha would spend time talking with the boy on each and every visit. Maybe Elisha taught him to play checkers in the little room the boy's parents had built for the prophet. Because the woman continued to show hospitality to Elisha, when the boy died of an apparent cerebral hemorrhage, God used Elisha to bring him back to life.

I believe his mother would probably delight in telling others of the blessing of hospitality.

I can envision readers saying, "Yes, but look at the second sentence in the story from Second Kings. She was a wealthy woman. If I were wealthy, I would get a pineapple and have it outside and polished all the time."

My father was a machinist in a factory. My mother never worked outside the home. When I was a teenager, there were seven of us in a three bedroom, one bath home...my parents, myself, three of my four older brothers, and one nephew. We were not poor, but neither were we rich. We always had deliciously-prepared, adequate meals. But there were never many leftovers.

It was our privilege to know a "man of God"…a modern day Elisha. His name was Rev. Button. He did open-air evangelism at fairs, festivals, and some bigger venues like the Indianapolis 500 car race. He drove all over the country sharing Jesus from a small camper that had been specially built with a staging area on the side from which he preached, did "chalk talks," and performed gospel magic.

Like the Shunammite woman and her husband, my parents let this man of God know that whenever he was anywhere near our home, the pineapple would be on the porch to welcome him. They could not build on a room for him. As the only girl, I occupied the only "single" room in the house. It was therefore simply understood that when Rev. Button came, I moved to the couch and he stayed in my room. I can remember getting off the bus and seeing Rev. Button's van in our driveway. My teenage brother and I would often break into a sprint saying excitedly, "Oh, look! Rev. Button is here!"

He talked to us. He played games with us. We got to play with the rabbits he would pull from his hat in his gospel magic act. He shared his deep love of Jesus with us. Sure the house was crowded for a couple days each time. Sure I had to sleep on the couch. But it didn't matter, because we got to be with this man of God.

Looking back, I have often wondered if, when Rev. Button would just appear at the door, (no cell phones with which to call ahead in those days) mom might have panicked over how to stretch the spaghetti to feed one more mouth. Or if my parents ever thought, "This is not a convenient time." If they did, they never let on. This was a man of God! It was their duty, but it was also a blessing to all of us to show him hospitality.

I believe that some day--in heaven--when crowns are passed out and people are recognized for faithfulness, my parents' names will be read and then God will say, "You get to share in the prize for each of the people Rev. Button led to Jesus during his life because you always made him feel welcome in your home."

CHAPTER 3

MARY OR MARTHA

In the church where I grew up, the ladies ministry group was called the Mary-Martha Ministry. Every year, at the mother/daughter banquet, someone would refer to the incident told about in Luke's gospel, chapter 10, verses 38-41. If, like me, you grew up in church, you know that this is the story of when Jesus came to dine in the home of Mary and Martha. During the yearly discussion of these verses, Martha always got a bum rap! She was overly concerned with cooking while Mary sat at Jesus feet learning from him. I always noticed though, that this discussion took place after we had devoured a delicious meal. As for me, I was always thankful that our church had some Marthas who were excellent cooks and that not everyone was just sitting attentively "at the feet of Jesus" (figuratively) learning while we all went hungry.

As an adult, when I looked more closely at this passage of scripture, I saw something never mentioned in my childhood. The Bible tells us in verse 38 that Martha welcomed Jesus and his disciples into her home. This is a very strange statement, when you think of the time period in which it was happening. Martha owned the home,....not Mary and not Lazarus. Knowing this gave me a deeper empathy for Martha. No wonder she was busy preparing food and making everything just right. It was HER home. She felt responsible. She was the original "Martha Stewart" type (no pun intended)....she wanted everything to be perfect for her special guest.

It has always been encouraging to me to see, as you continue through the gospel narrative, that Jesus returned to Martha's home many times after that initial visit. He didn't give up on her after his famous "Martha, Martha...you are upset over all these things--Mary has chosen the better way" discourse. I wonder if in the other visits, Jesus might have gone into the kitchen to help Martha. Knowing her personality, as only the Son of God could, perhaps he understood that she could "learn of him" better if he taught in her domain.

18

When I was a child, I always idolized missionaries. But I did not truly know any until a family who were missionaries to Ethiopia came to visit our church. There was a man, his wife, and six children. There was a girl just about my age in the family. Imagine my excitement and joy when my mom invited them to our house for supper. I was going to get to know MISSIONARIES.

Being a bit of a Martha, even at a young age, I wanted everything to be perfect. I fussed around about how their family of 8 and our family of 5 (at that point) would ever fit around our dining room table. Mom solved that by saying some of us would eat in the kitchen. I was worried about how that would look.

Soon they arrived. I thought we should all sit in the living room and discuss the lost heathens in Ethiopia. Imagine my surprise when Mom invited Mrs. Fellows to come into the kitchen and help with the meal preparations. But Theresa Fellows was thrilled to be made to feel so welcome. When Mom was mashing the potatoes (how many potatoes does one cook for 13 people anyway?) the youngest girl in the Fellows family whispered something in her mother's ear. With a laugh,

Theresa asked my Mom if little Karen could lick the beaters after the potatoes were mashed. That is the day that missionaries came off the pedestal in my mind and became very real people like us with all the same problems and joys...people who loved Jesus so much that they gave up family and friends to go to Africa to serve Him. Someone in our church wanted to buy Mr. Fellows a new suit. He told them that he had a suit and they should put their money into missions work. I was impacted by these people through my parent's hospitality!

Many years passed, the little Martha (me) had grown up, married, had children of my own, and moved into a new town. We were looking for a church to attend, a process which always irritated me. How do you know whether God wants you in one church or another, after all? Do you base it on music, preaching style, friendliness of the people,....what? When we sat down in the new church, I warily opened the bulletin. My eyes fell on a special paragraph that said they were pleased to welcome into the pulpit today Rev. Alex Fellows, missionary to Ethiopia. I was overjoyed! The first missionaries I ever knew were here! And he was going to preach. When the service was over, I approached Theresa Fellows cautiously.

"You probably don't remember me, but.." I stammered.

She grabbed me in a hug and said, "Why, you are Raelene Wood! I remember you and your family well. Your mom let our little Karen lick the mashed potatoes off the beaters. She really had the gift of hospitality!"

I told Theresa that we were looking for a church home since we had just moved to this city. She hugged me again and said, "You have just found a wonderful church. They have supported us for years. This congregation will love you to death." She was right. Four of the happiest years of our lives were spent attending that church.

It has been our joy since that time to entertain Alex and Theresa in our home several times. They are some of God's choice servants, and I feel it is a special privilege to know them. I am thankful that Mom had the heart of Mary and Martha combined when she put the pineapple on the porch to welcome them into our home.

CHAPTER 4

A BEAUTIFUL DAY IN THE NEIGHBORHOOD

W hen my children were small, they often watched a children's television program which began with the star of the show singing "It's a beautiful day in the neighborhood, a beautiful day for a neighbor, would you be mine?" I remember often thinking that the days when people got together and socialized with their neighbors were gone forever. Oh, we spoke to our neighbors and sometimes the children played together. But, as far as developing any kind of lasting friendships like those portrayed on that television program—it just didn't happen.

Then we moved to Delaware, Ohio. My husband was out of full time pastoral ministry at that time. He had chosen to leave the ministry because he had lost his love of people. He felt that God could use him in a different arena—the United States military. And so, he had become a full time

Ohio National Guardsman. It was at this point in time that we moved to Ravine Ridge Drive, a lovely quiet neighborhood in the small town which is a suburb of the capitol of Ohio.

When you move because of a new assignment in the ministry, you immediately have lots of new friends. In fact, it can be almost overwhelming as you try to learn the names of all the people in your new church. They only have to remember two new names, while the pastor and his wife have to learn nearly one hundred...plus sort out who is related to whom!

But, as I said, this move was different. We did not have an instant church family. I wondered how we would make any friends. Dan's comrades at the Armory were scattered all over the greater Columbus, Ohio area. But I needn't have worried.

We moved into our home on a Tuesday afternoon. On Wednesday evening, our doorbell rang. Dan answered the door as I stood in the bedroom trying to decide where to hang a picture. I heard him say, "Come in." I wondered who would be visiting us since we didn't know a soul in Delaware. I ran a brush through my hair quickly and headed for the living room.

That is when I met Wayne and Garnelle Lloyd. They were smiling from ear to ear and both stood to shake my hand. I judged them to be in their early seventies, basing this solely upon his receding hairline and her impeccable manners—the kind taught in the "old school." We discovered that they were our neighbors who lived three doors down. Dan handed me a piece of paper which I soon discovered was a printed invitation to a party which they would be giving in their home on Friday evening.

"Oh, we so hope that you can come," Garnelle said. "It will be a carry-in dinner of sorts…but we don't want you two to bring anything but yourselves. Please say you'll come. All the neighbors want to meet you."

There was no way we could refuse this dear couple. Wayne said, "We came here first to make sure the time and date suited you folks. If it does, we will go and invite the others."

After another round of handshakes and a shy hug from Garnelle, they left. We stared at each other dumbstruck. It was getting dark, so we could stand back from the window a bit and remain undetected. We watched as they went from door to door and invited all the neighbors on the block.

That Friday evening was a hallmark event in our lives. Nearly everyone was there. They all wanted to know about us and what brought us to Delaware. They laughed and told stories about each other. The food was delicious and the women readily shared their recipes. They welcomed us into the neighborhood with open arms. They encouraged us to come and see them. "Yell if you need anything!" "We are all like a big family," they said.

From that day on, whenever we were outside we would hear a friendly, "Hi Dan! How are you, Raelene?" No one ever crossed the line to become pests. They were just our friends. We knew that if we needed them, they would be there. Sometimes when the dog days of summer came, we would visit on each other's porches. Lemonade was consumed by the gallon while friendships grew.

As we became more deeply acquainted with the other people on the block, we discovered that it was the hospitality of Wayne and Garnelle Lloyd that cemented us all together. They had thrown a "Welcome to the Neighborhood Party" for each of the other families on their first Friday night on the block. This dear couple certainly had their pineapple on the porch—not only to people they knew, but to the strangers who moved in.

We lived four of the happiest years of our lives there on Ravine Ridge Drive in Delaware. But then came the sad day when Wayne and Garnelle came to tell us they were going to move. None of us could believe it. Even though we knew they were just going across town, we clung to them and wept.

I remember the day the moving van drove past our house, with the Lloyds following closely in their car. I stood at the window and waved, with tears dripping off my face. As I glanced across the street, the lady who lived there was doing the same. Shortly after they pulled away, five of us stood in the middle of the street wiping tears and saying, "It will never be the same around here."

We were right. When the new people moved into the Lloyds home, we invited them to come to our home to meet the other neighbors. They were always too busy and didn't seem to want to get involved.

One by one we watched as the other families put their homes up for sale and also moved away. One couple moved to be closer to their children. The young family across from us moved to be closer to his work. Another couple went into a retirement community. The beautiful day in our neighborhood had ended.

Looking back, I have often thought of the dynamics that made those such happy days. There were vast differences in our ages. Some of us were Christian, some were not. Some were white collar, some were blue collar. Some were retired. Others worked long hours. Some had pets, others did not. One family had children living at home. What glued us together in lifelong friendships was the love and acceptance of Wayne and Garnelle Lloyd. They were not Bible scholars. They might not even know that in 1 Peter 4:9 we are instructed to "Use hospitality one to another without grudging." (King James Version) They probably don't know the historical significance of the pineapple and how it represents open hearts and open doors. They just love people and know how to entertain in a gentle, quiet way. When I grow up, I want to be like them!

28

CHAPTER 5

A SMASHED PINEAPPLE

Some people may not wish to extend hospitality to others because they remember a time in their lives when someone smashed their pineapple.

Each year, when our children were small, we would spend time with them carving a jack-o-lantern out of a pumpkin to place on our porch for Halloween. They enjoyed this immensely and would happily remind us each evening to light the candle inside the jack-o-lantern so it would illuminate the porch. One morning, I heard a shriek from my daughter when she went out to play on the swing set. She came back inside in tears saying, "Somebody smashed my pumpkin!" Sure enough, our street was littered with jack-o-lantern pieces in front of each house where the day before there had been the happy face of a little Halloween friend. Obviously, some unruly

29

teenagers had decided a Halloween prank was more fun than seeing the lighted jack-o-lanterns line the street. I remember finding it hard to explain this to a sobbing four year old. I told her that they didn't understand that she loved the little jack-o-lantern and they just wanted to do their own thing. Selfishness was the problem, I explained.

Many years later, our pastor announced in service that the next week we would be having a Sunday evening concert performed by a very famous Christian pianist. He went on to say that he wanted to give someone in the congregation the opportunity to use their gift of hospitality and have this man spend Sunday night in their home. Remembering all the good times I had growing up in a home where the pineapple was always on the porch, I eagerly approached my husband with the idea of entertaining this man. He agreed, with the stipulation that he hoped the man enjoyed basketball as the Chicago Bulls would be in a play-off game that evening.

The concert was wonderful. He spoke eloquently about his love of the Lord between each song. He seemed to be a wonderful servant of Jesus who had dedicated his talent to bring glory and honor to God.

At the close of the service, there was a line of people waiting to purchase his tapes and compact discs. They wanted to get his autograph and have a chance to speak with him. Dan and I had prearranged that I would rush home and prepare a simple meal to serve while Dan stayed behind. I remember singing "Great is thy Faithfulness" as I set the table and cooked. I was reheating a dish of roast beef in the microwave. The corn was beginning to boil on the stove. Just as I was checking to see if the potatoes were ready to be mashed, Dan and our guest arrived. Dan took him to the guest room and showed him where he could hang his things. In a few minutes, he came into the kitchen.

"Oh, this will never do!" he stated matter-of-factly. "I want a Turkey Bacon Club sandwich."

Can you imagine my surprise, quickly followed by (I am ashamed to say) my complete indignation? Who did he think he was? I had labored to make a simple, but hearty meal for our special guest. But here he stood saying, "No—I won't eat this. I need a Turkey Bacon Club."

I stuttered, "But I don't have any turkey."

31

His reply was simple. "Is there a fast food restaurant nearby where I can get a Turkey Bacon Club sandwich?"

Within minutes, Dan and our guest left to go to the nearest sandwich shop to purchase what he felt he needed. I stayed behind to clean up the kitchen, to mash potatoes and then immediately put them in the refrigerator for us to eat the next day. I was irate, but still determined to be a good hostess.

Michael Jordan was playing with the Chicago Bulls back then. We rarely ever missed watching him on TV. Michael was poetry in motion on a basketball court. Both Dan and I loved his games. So while the men were still out and I was still 'fuming', I decided to turn on the game.

Upon their return, Dan immediately wanted to know the score and asked, "How many points has MJ scored?"

Whereupon our guest informed us, "This will never do. The Tony Awards for Broadway musicals are being broadcast tonight and I need to see them."

I was so very tempted to lie and tell him that we did not receive the channel on our TV which was playing the Tony Award program—but I never got the chance. For he had spied the remote to the TV and switched the channel to what he wanted to see!

Dan picked up the newspaper and read every line of it...or was he just hiding his agitation with the pianist behind it? After about half an hour, I declared that I was tired and would go to bed. I informed Mr. Pianist that we would both be leaving for work by 7:30 AM. "I will set out what you need for breakfast and you can just lock the door as you leave," I stated.

Never taking his eyes from the Tony Awards, he waved his hand at me and said, "Just put out an assortment of cereal, bagels with cream cheese, and some fruit. That will be fine."

I have often wondered (with a wicked grin on my face!) if he was surprised the next morning when he found a bowl, a spoon, a box of Cheerios, and a loaf of bread by the toaster.

Obviously, this was not a good experience. This man literally SMASHED my pineapple. But, should one bad guest rule the rest of my life? Should I refuse to EVER entertain anyone else because of his rudeness? Wouldn't I be missing many potential blessings if I allowed myself to think back to this experience rather than to the good ones?

We have since had many laughs over that fiasco. Our daughter has since had many laughs over her smashed pumpkin and how it had been the best one she had ever carved. But, guess what? She still decorates her home for Halloween and other holidays. I'm thankful that she does not let one bad experience rule the rest of her life. Like her, I am trying to learn that one bad experience with a selfish person is not cause to put my pineapple away forever.

CHAPTER 6

BUT NOT NOW LORD

God graciously called my husband and me back into full time pastoral ministry after a time in our lives when we had been pursuing secular careers. We felt He was giving us a 'second chance' to serve Him with our whole hearts. We were thrilled beyond measure when a small country church called us to come and be their pastoral family. It was an exciting time, but my excitement was dampened (literally) with the tears of goodbye as we moved and left our friends. Even now, next to my desk in the parsonage, there is a lovely cross-stitched piece made by my dear friend from our former home, Connie. Across the top it says Friendship Memories. Ladies of that church signed it at my going away party. I often find myself looking at it and remembering the time we spent with them.

But, the call of God had been so distinct.

35

I moved into the parsonage and began to get acquainted with our new congregation. People could not understand why I was frightened to live on Cowpath Road out in the middle of nowhere. This city bred girl had never been fearful in Chicago or the other cities in which we had lived. But great expanses of open fields and not seeing any other lights in the evening had me thoroughly spooked. The ladies of our church laughed at me. I felt like the proverbial fish out of water.

Perhaps that is why Connie's call meant so much to me. My old church was having a women's retreat. "Can you come?" she asked excitedly. "We'll share a room and we can talk all night. It'll be like old times."

I think my husband could tell that my head had made the move to our new church but my heart was still working to catch up. "Sure," he said. "Why don't you plan to go? It'll be good for you to get away for a few days…back where things are more familiar." Excitedly, I planned for the trip. What I would wear, what time I would leave, when I would return. I even made a list of things to remember to tell Connie.

The big day finally arrived and I didn't even

feel guilty as I thought, "I'm going home." Then my husband dropped the bomb shell on me. Nonchalantly he said, "You do remember that on Saturday afternoon we have missionaries coming to stay with us, don't you?"

"What?" I exploded. "You know I will not be getting any sleep on Friday night and I will come home exhausted. What do you mean they are going to stay with us? And who are they anyway?" Tears were just beneath the surface.

"Now, honey," he implored. "Don't get upset! I'm sure I told you about this. Before we ever came here, the denomination had already set up this missions conference. The people's names are Bob and Donna Eagle. They are missionaries to the Dominican Republic. They'll get here Saturday afternoon some time and be staying with us till Monday. But don't you worry about a thing. Just go ahead and go to your retreat."

Only a man would think that when we were going to have houseguests for two nights…(six meals,…snacks to serve in the evenings…clean sheets needed on the bed) that I could go away and enjoy myself. I continued to whine.

"Danny—how could you? You NEVER told

me about this. I need to clean the house. I need to prepare food. I'll call Connie…"

"No, you won't!" he said as he took my overnight bag to the car. "I'll clean the house. We'll eat out. I know how you have been looking forward to this."

I didn't let the matter drop there. I went the whole nine yards! "Why do they have to stay with US? Why can't they stay with one of the deacons? Why…"

But I could tell by the look on his face that this matter was non-negotiable. He calmly explained that since we lived in a four bedroom parsonage, with two of those rooms unoccupied, there was no way he would ask someone else in the church to entertain the missionaries. "Anyway, we'll have fun!"

"You don't even know these people!" I countered. "They're probably old and boring and…"

By now he was literally pushing me toward the door telling me it would be okay and that I should get going on my retreat and to have fun.

Of course I fussed with God all the way to our old home town. And then I fussed to Connie that evening. Mostly, though, I fussed within myself. I was a mess!

Our wonderful gracious God knew just what I needed. Can you guess what the retreat speaker spoke about? Yielding ourselves to be used as God's instruments, given to hospitality! By the close of the retreat I had told God I was sorry and told Connie that God had made me see the situation in a new light. I was actually anxious to get back home and apologize to Dan.

I had been home from the retreat for exactly ten minutes...just long enough to tell my dear husband (who had the house 'spit-shined') how sorry I was...when the doorbell rang. Had there really been a pineapple to place on the porch, I wouldn't have even had time to get it out yet!

Into our lives walked Bob and Donna Eagle. Within ten minutes, we all were laughing uncontrollably. Within half an hour, the four of us were all holding hands praying through tears for our children. You see, Bob and Donna not only walked into our lives, they walked into our hearts. We share so many common interests it is unbelievable. Donna and I both love to read and can spend hours talking about the latest books

39

we have 'devoured.' Dan and Bob are both sports nuts and their banter over whether Ohio State or Michigan has the best football team is hilarious. We became such fast friends that I never even thought about the house or food that weekend. We played games, talked, ate, talked, talked some more, and bonded together like glue. As Donna says, we are truly "kindred spirits." When they left on Monday afternoon, Donna and I were crying and asking the guys how soon we could get together again? Our friendship developed to the place that the next year Dan and I realized a lifelong dream when we were able to go to the mission field in the Dominican Republic to visit them. Dan was able to preach in a church there, through an interpreter...and God met us in a special way that morning. A beautiful Dominican lady accepted Christ as her Savior.

What if I had refused to put my pineapple in the correct place that Saturday afternoon? What if I had said, "Lord, you know I like to be hospitable... but this is just not a convenient time!" Not only would we have been robbed of one of the most precious friendships we cherish, but maybe...just maybe...that dear woman from the Dominican Republic would not have been touched to ask Jesus to come into her heart.

So now, when the time does not seem just right for me, I try to remember this incident and get the pineapple all shined up and put it on the porch even then. **Hospitality just might have eternal consequences.**

CHAPTER 7

THE BASICS

Some will say, "OK...I can see that there is a Biblical mandate to be hospitable. I can see that there are blessings that come from being hospitable. I can see that even if I have a bad experience and get my figurative pineapple smashed, I should not let that rule my life. I understand that I should try to blend the personalities of Mary and Martha to be a good host or hostess. I can even see that I should entertain people at times when it is not especially convenient for me. But...help! I don't know how!" This chapter is for you. Some of the suggestions will seem so elementary that you will think, "Who does this author think she is talking to...a young child?" But I intend to share with you just a few of the things I do that makes entertaining guests very simple...things that our guests have commented about in notes after they leave our home.

43

When you are entertaining someone overnight, or, for an extended visit, it is wonderful if you can put them in a guest room, i.e. a room that is not occupied by someone else when there are no guests. (If you reread chapter two, you will note that this was not possible in my family's home when I was growing up. DO NOT let this stop you from entertaining. You can incorporate the following suggestions after your child gets all his/her "stuff" out of the room that is to be occupied by the guest.) Whatever your situation, here are a few hints to make the guest's room a home away from home for them:

§ Make sure there is a mirror in the room. Tell your guest to feel free to place their toiletries on a table, dresser, or stand near the mirror. Place the mirror near an easily visible electrical outlet---this will facilitate curling irons, hairdryers, and electric razors usage. (If the guest is to have their own private bathroom, this is not quite as necessary... but a mirror in the guest room is still a good idea.)

§ Make sure the windows have room darkening shades of some kind. If there is likely to be any question, show your guest how to work the shades.

§ Make sure there is something in the guest room upon which they can place their suitcase, other than the floor. We happen to have a suitcase holder much like what nice motels have. You can often pick these up at garage sales or auctions and they are not very expensive. However, a TV tray or even just a heavy box with a pretty towel on top will work just as well. When you show them to their room say, "You can place your suitcase here."

§ If possible, clear a bit of space in a closet and tell your guest, "You can hang clothes in here."

§ Make sure there is a chair in the room. This can be anything from a nice overstuffed chair, which you pick up at a sale, to a metal folding chair. Most people prefer to sit on a chair instead of a bed when tying their shoes.

§ If at all possible, have a fairly firm mattress on the bed. People who are used to sleeping on soft beds can usually sleep on a firmer one without ill effects. However, those who need a firm mattress may not be able to walk after sleeping on a super soft bed. A piece of plywood placed under the mattress is an inexpensive way to care for this need.

§   Purchase a cheap alarm clock which you place on a bedside table so your guest can determine when he or she wishes to get up in the morning. You might want to tell them to feel free to use the clock. Give instructions on how to work it if necessary.

§   A lamp on the bedside table that can be reached from the bed is a must. Shop garage sales.

§   If you do not have a bedside table, go to any discount store and pick up one of the round fiberboard tables with three screw-in legs from the "Domestics" department (less than $10). Cover with a piece of cloth. Voila!

§   If your guest will not have their own private bathroom, place sets of matching towels on the foot of the guest bed. Hint: Make sure you launder brand new towels first so the fuzzies will not come off all over your guest upon use. Use extra fabric softener in the rinse to make them smell especially inviting. (If the guests are to have use of a private bath, you can place the towels in the bathroom... again, make sure you tell them "These are your towels".) We have cheap towel rods on the inside of guest room doors and extras in the bathroom so there is no question as to what to do with the towels after usage.

Now for some of the little "extras" to make your guest feel welcome:

§   Keep a few magazines on the bedside table in the guest room. My favorites are *Good Housekeeping* for women, *Time* for men, or *Reader's Digest* for both. In the Christian market, I would choose *Virtue* for women, *Leadership* for men, or *Guideposts* for both.

§   A scented candle already burning when you show your guests to their room is nice. A book of matches placed beside the candle will let them know that they can feel free to light it again.

§   Flowers or a green plant is an extra special touch.

§   When you travel, save the small toiletries from the motels and place them in a basket in your guest room. Be sure to tell them to feel free to use these items. Many women like to try a different shampoo or hand cream, so even if they have brought their own they will take you up on this offer.

§   We keep a Guest Book in our guest room and ask each visitor who spends a night with us to sign it.

Now a few hints about your actions that will either make a guest <u>feel</u> at home or make them wish they had <u>stayed</u> at home.

§   Keep the TV turned <u>OFF</u> unless it is something that you and your guests will enjoy watching together. There is <u>NOTHING</u> as rude as a host or hostess who insists on keeping a TV on and then tries to talk over the sound. The excuse, "I just keep it on for the noise" does not make any sense when you have guests.

§ Be yourself. If you normally slip into pajamas and robe during the evening, go ahead and do so and tell your guests to feel free to do the same. If you normally take your shoes off, do so and tell your guests to feel free to do the same.

§ Be sensitive to your guests comfort. Ask them if they are too warm or too cold. You can turn the heat or air conditioning up or down to suit their needs. As the host or hostess, you can either put on or take off layers to accommodate the change from your usual thermostat setting. The guest will likely not have that same option. Don't say, "I keep my house cool, so cover up with this afghan if you are cold." Adjust your usual settings to their needs. (A couple days at a different setting will make virtually no change in your utility bills.)

§ Also be sensitive to 'special' needs of your guests. My mother is blind in one eye and has macular degeneration in the other. Her doctor has told her that the only answer for her poor sight is lots of bright light. When she visits in our home, as evening approaches, we turn on every light in the living room. We also make sure the hallway light is on. We do this nonchalantly, not making a big issue of it. Her needs come ahead of ours.

§   This also carries over to watching TV or a video with someone who has poor hearing. Ask them if they can hear…and make necessary adjustments. Better for it to be a bit too loud for your ears than for a guest to be forced to sit and stare at something they cannot hear or understand.

Perhaps the most logical advice for any host/hostess is found in the words of Jesus, which we call the Golden Rule, found in Matthew 7:12. (New Living Translation) "Do for others what you would like them to do for you." The Message puts it even more clearly. "Here is a simple rule-of-thumb for behavior: Ask yourself what you want people to do for you, then grab the initiative and do it for them." In other words, put yourself in the guests' shoes. Think of things that would make you either more or less comfortable when visiting in someone else's home. Act accordingly.

CHAPTER 8

A WORD ABOUT FOOD

I n most evangelical Christian circles we have come to equate the word hospitality with food. We tend to think that the more elaborate the spread of food we offer to a guest, the more welcome they will feel. When you think about it, we haven't learned a lot in the 200 plus years since America's infancy. Back then, people thought that if you really wanted to impress your guest you had to have a pineapple. Even if it was a rented pineapple which you could not cut, they knew you cared if you made the effort to have the exotic fruit. In today's culture this could be translated into many different practices. Some people think that to entertain guests at a meal they must purchase the most expensive cuts of meat, have elaborate desserts, give a choice of vegetables, breads, salads, etc. In short, people think that to entertain guests they have to go to a lot of trouble, cost, and bother. Nothing could be further from the truth.

I remember when my husband was away serving with the United States military. One Sunday a friend from church asked if I would like to come and eat with their family. I was so thrilled not to have to go back to that empty house and try to find something that would be appetizing to eat alone! When we arrived at their home, my hostess told me, "We always have the same thing for Sunday lunch. I hope you enjoy Campbell's tomato soup and toasted cheese sandwiches." I admit that I was a bit surprised, but I felt very wanted and very at home at their table. They introduced me to the idea of "dunking" my toasted cheese sandwich in my tomato soup. I had never heard of this practice, but it is one I do to this day. With fond memories of a hostess who cared more about the fact that I was going to be eating alone that day than she did about her lack of anything fancy to serve me, I dunk away! (By the way, don't knock it if you haven't tried it.) It was at this impromptu lunch that I learned the truth of the old saying: "A crumb in the home of friends is better than a cake eaten alone."

I have learned that my guests are more comfortable if it does not look as though I have worked myself into a tizzy to fix food for them. With that in mind, I try to do as much food preparation in advance of their arrival as possible. My motto has become **K.I.S.S.** (Keep it simple, stupid!)

This simplicity has carried over into every area of eating at our home. I have often become so bogged down when a charming hostess says something like "What would you like to drink? We have iced tea (either sweet or plain), Pepsi, lemonade, Root Beer, grape Kool-aid, milk, chocolate milk, coffee (decaf or regular), Seven Up, ice water, hot tea..." Well, you get the point. When we have guests at our home for dinner, I give everyone ice water with their meal. When and if I serve dessert, I offer decaf coffee. If there are children, I will have milk or lemonade. Rather than giving them the same list of choices offered in smorgasbords, I keep it simple...even when it comes to drinks. When guests stay with us for a day or more, naturally I will widen their choices for drinks a bit. I also will have some caffeinated and some decaffeinated drinks, keeping in mind that many people are unknowingly addicted to caffeine.

Before I share some simple recipes with you, let me say a word about dietary requirements. When guests will be staying for a day or more, it is a common courtesy for the hostess to ask if they have any special dietary needs. The one that is preeminent in my mind is whether or not people can have sugar. I know that some diabetics control their disease with insulin. I also know that I do not want to serve anything to someone who has diabetes or hypoglycemia which may send them to the hospital. It is so simple to avoid sugar in desserts since the introduction of fat-free, sugar-free puddings. You can fill a pie crust with any of these, adding either natural fruits or fruits canned only in their own juices (rather than heavy syrup). I have never had anything but rave reviews for pies fixed in this way. No one can tell that there is no sugar involved, unless I tell them. A large grocery will also have a few sugar free cakes, cookies, etc. in their bakery. I purchase these when I don't know if someone is sensitive to sugar in foods. No one has ever been able to tell when something is sugar free. Better safe than sorry.

Because of some food allergies and health problems in our family, I have learned NEVER to try to force someone to eat something. No matter how good something tastes, it is not worth making your guest take another dose of medicine to counteract what you have made them feel obligated to taste with remarks such as, "Oh...just taste it. Surely a little bit won't hurt you." In some cases, a little bit can be fatal. Don't embarrass your guest with food.

Some of my favorite recipes are ones that can be done in advance and served quickly. I often stay up a few minutes after my guests go to bed to get the food started for the next day. When that is not practical, I set my alarm for an hour before everyone else will be up and do as much as possible in advance. Here are some quick, easy favorites that are stand-bys in my recipe file.

Breakfast or Brunch Strata

12 slices of white bread, cubed

2 cups of shredded cheese

8 eggs

2 cups of ham cubed

1 cup chopped onion

1 teaspoon salt

4 cups milk

¼ teaspoon pepper

Place bread cubes in buttered 9 X 13 dish. On top of bread, layer onion, ham, and cheese. Beat eggs, milk, and seasonings and pour over this. Bake at 350 degrees for 45 to 50 minutes.
Serves 8.

Beef Stroganoff

Put a 2 pound roast beef in a crockpot 36 hours before you want to eat. Cover with water, season with salt and pepper. Cook on low. On the 2nd morning, pour off all but 1 cup of the broth. Cut beef into tiny bits, removing any fat and bones. Add 1 can of onion soup and 2 cans of cream of mushroom soup. Stir well. Continue to cook on low all day. One hour before serving, stir in one cup of sour cream. Serve over minute rice, noodles, or biscuits.

Hint: You can use the most inexpensive cut of roast for this. Cooking it for 36 hours will make ANY beef so tender it falls apart. You can also substitute plain yogurt for sour cream in any recipe...this brings the fat grams down and makes it more easily digested by anyone with a lactose tolerance problem.

Chicken Bacon Wrap Ups

8-12 boneless, skinless chicken breasts

1 large package Buddig dried beef (shred)

8-12 slices bacon

1 can Cream of Mushroom soup

1 cup sour cream (I substitute plain yogurt)

Line greased 9 x 13 pan with shredded dried beef. Wrap each chicken breast with bacon slices and lay on beef. Mix soup and sour cream (or yogurt) and pour over. Cover and refrigerate overnight. Uncover and bake at 275 degrees for 3 hours. Do not add seasonings.

(This recipe was given to me by my dear friend, Jan Storms. Her pineapple is always in the most prominent place on her porch. Thanks for always showing us hospitality, Jan!)

Crock Pot Beef Stew

1 ½ pounds beef cubes (can be frozen)

1 medium onion chopped

3 medium potatoes chopped

1 pound bag frozen mixed vegetables

8 oz tomato sauce

16 oz water

2 Tablespoons flour

salt and pepper

Dump everything into a crockpot (remember meat and veggies can be frozen!) Cook on high 6-8 hours. Stir. Add water if necessary to make gravy.

(Our friend Candy Jackson served this beef stew to my husband and me a mere 45 minutes after she had come in from a full days work. It is a no-fail recipe that takes away all excuses for not being hospitable because you are too busy. I have used it many times. Thank you, Candy!)

Lazy Day Overnight Lasagna

1 pound mild sausage or ground beef

1 32 oz jar of prepared spaghetti sauce

1 8 oz can tomato sauce

1 cup water

1 16 oz carton cottage cheese

2 tablespoons chopped chives

½ teaspoon dried oregano leaves

1 egg

1 16 oz package sliced mozzarella cheese

2 tablespoons grated parmesan cheese

8 oz uncooked lasagna noodles

Brown meat—drain well. Add spaghetti sauce, tomato sauce, and water, blend well. Simmer five minutes. In medium bowl combine cottage cheese, chives, oregano and egg—mix well. In bottom of ungreased 9 X 13 pan, spread 1½ cups of the meat sauce, top with half of the uncooked noodles, half of cheese mix, and half of mozzarella. Repeat with remaining noodles, cottage cheese mix and mozzarella cheese. Top with remaining meat sauce. Sprinkle with parmesan cheese. Cover and refrigerate overnight.

Bake uncovered at 350 degrees for 50 to 60 minutes or until noodles are tender and casserole is bubbly. Cover and let stand 15 minutes before serving.

(This recipe is popular among military families because it is cheap, hearty, and takes little time to prepare. We first ate this in Germany when we visited our son at the Karlsruhe Army base.)

Creamy Hash Brown Casserole

Begin with a 2 lb package of frozen hash brown potatoes which you will let thaw ½ hour. While the potatoes are thawing, melt ¼ cup margarine in very large bowl in microwave. To this, add one can cream of chicken soup and ½ cup diced onions. Add one pound carton of sour cream (I substitute plain yogurt.) Add 8 oz. grated sharp cheese. Add some salt and pepper to taste. Stir the thawed hash brown potatoes into the other ingredients in the bowl. Place all in a greased 9x13 pan. Cover top of casserole with crushed potato chips. Bake at 350 degrees for one hour.

Hint: This works best with the hash brown potatoes that are in cubes rather than shredded.

(In our first pastorate, our head deacon's wife served this casserole to our family. Our children loved it and it became a favorite at every holiday. I often bring it to church carry-in dinners. Thank you, Lois, for using your home to entertain our family on many occasions.)

I could list many other recipes, but I hope you get the picture. "Keep it simple" is a wonderful motto. With each of the dishes I have listed, there is minimal preparation which needs to be done just before serving. This allows you to enjoy visiting with your guests. What fun to be able to chat with them, excuse yourself to the kitchen for just a few minutes, and then call them to the table to enjoy a happy meal with a non-frazzled host or hostess.

Dan has taken on the task of clearing away the guests' dinnerware while I fix dessert...which usually is nothing more elaborate than cutting a pie or cake or placing cookies in a bowl. He serves the dessert while I pour the coffee and quickly stack dishes in the sink, rejoining my guests to enjoy the simple dessert with them.

My husband and I have agreed that if we have guests in for dinner he will keep the conversation flowing while I quickly refrigerate anything that requires it after our meal. Then we retire to the living room and relax. After the guests leave, he helps me with scraping, rinsing, and loading the dishwasher. No one spends any time in the kitchen during our visit. Dan and I have discovered it is rewarding to relive the fun times while we work together to clear the table and clean up. The dishwasher is started when we go to bed.

CHAPTER 9

MY PRAYER FOR YOU

All of my immediate family has been scattered far and wide. Though I have four older brothers and a living mother and step-father, no one lives closer than sixty miles to me. Our extended family reaches from the east coast to the west coast and from Florida to Ohio. So the times that some of us get to see each other are rare.

My brother, David, is 2½ years older than me. Though we love each other dearly, we have always fussed with each other—sometimes rather dramatically. There were times when we were small that I am sure mom and dad despaired of ever raising both of us alive. We fought hard and played hard. And we scrapped continually. Yet there are times when I would give anything to be able to see him.

Last summer, David and his dear wife, Linda,

and their young adult daughters, Joann and Sara, visited us overnight in our home. Dan and I tried to incorporate every technique described in this book while playing host and hostess to them.nnImagine my surprise when I found that my brother (who picks on me unmercifully) left this note in our guest book: "Beautiful house! Great church! Hospitality! A great time!" After they returned to Florida, my sister-in-law and each of my nieces wrote a thank you note to us in which they also commented on our wonderful hospitality. They could not have paid us a higher compliment.

That is why there is a slate sign on the front door of our home. At the top, in beautiful script, is the word WELCOME! Underneath the word is a simple but very clear painting of—you guessed it! A pineapple!

It is my prayer that you will find your pineapple, shine it all up, and place it in a very prominent place near the entrance of your home. If you cannot do this literally, I pray you will do it in your heart.

To Contact Raelene Phillips for
speaking engagements please write:

Raelene Phillips
9310 Cowpath Rd
St. Paris, OH 43072